It's Catching

Strep Throat

Elizabeth Laskey

Heinemann Library
Chicago, Illinois

Designed by Patricia Stevenson
Printed and bound in the United States by Lake Book Manufacturing

07 06 05 04 03
10 9 8 7 6 5 4 3 2 1

Library of Congress Cataloging-in-Publication Data
Laskey, Elizabeth, 1961–
    Strep throat / Elizabeth Laskey.
        v. cm. — (It's catching)
    Includes bibliographical references and index.
    Contents: What is strep throat? — Healthy nose and throat —
    What causes strep throat? — First signs — Other signs — Sore throats —
    Finding out — How strep throat is spread — Treatment — Getting better —
    Avoiding strep throat — Staying healthy — Think about it.
    ISBN 1-4034-0276-0
    1. Streptococcal infections—Juvenile literature.
    2. Throat—Diseases—Juvenile literature.
    [1. Streptococcal infections. 2. Throat—Diseases. 3. Diseases.]
    I. Title. II. Series.n

    RC116.S84 L37 2002
    616.9'2—dc21
                            2001008567

Acknowledgments
The author and publishers are grateful to the following for permission to reproduce copyright material:
Cover photograph by Michael Newman/PhotoEdit
p. 4 Chris Lowe/Index Stock Imagery/PictureQuest; p. 5 Jeff Isaac Greenberg/Photo Researchers, Inc.; pp. 6, 25 Custom Medical Stock Photo, Inc.; p. 7 Stephen Welstead/Corbis Stock Market; p. 8 Oliver Meckes/Photo Researchers, Inc.; p. 9 Stevie Grand/Science Photo Library/Photo Researchers, Inc.; p. 10 Wally McNamee/Corbis; p. 11 John Henley/Corbis Stock Market; p. 12 Gabe Palmer/Corbis Stock Market; p. 13 Dr. P. Marazzi/Science Photo Library/Photo Researchers, Inc.; p. 14 Bob Daemmrich/Stock Boston, Inc.; p. 15 Ken Cavanagh/Photo Researchers, Inc.; p. 16 Billy E. Barnes/PhotoEdit/PictureQuest; p. 17 Stephen Frisch/Stock Boston, Inc.; p. 18 Tom Bannor/Custom Medical Stock Photo, Inc.; p. 19 Yoav Levy/PhotoTake; p. 20 Ed Bock/Corbis Stock Market; p. 21 Mark Richards/PhotoEdit; p. 22 Mary Steinbacher/PhotoEdit; p. 23 Mike Bluestone/Science Photo Library/Photo Researchers, Inc.; p. 24 The Image Bank/Getty Images; p. 26 Greg Nikas/Corbis; p. 27 Robert Hauser/Index Stock Imagery/PictureQuest; p. 28 Margaret Ross/Stock Boston, Inc./PictureQuest; p. 29 Dennis MacDonald/PhotoEdit.
Every effort has been made to contact copyright holders of any material reproduced in this book. Any omissions will be rectified in subsequent printings if notice is given to the publisher.

Some words are shown in bold, **like this.** You can find out what they mean by looking in the glossary.

Contents

What Is Strep Throat?

Strep throat is a sickness that makes your throat hurt a lot. Most of the time strep throat is not serious, but it can make you feel very sick.

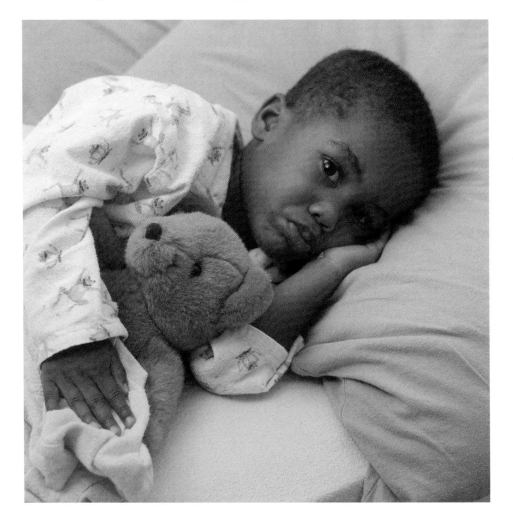

Strep throat is an **infectious** illness. This means it can spread from one person to another.

Healthy Nose and Throat

Your nose and throat help protect you from **germs.** A healthy throat is the color pink. Your nose and throat have sticky insides called **mucous membranes.**

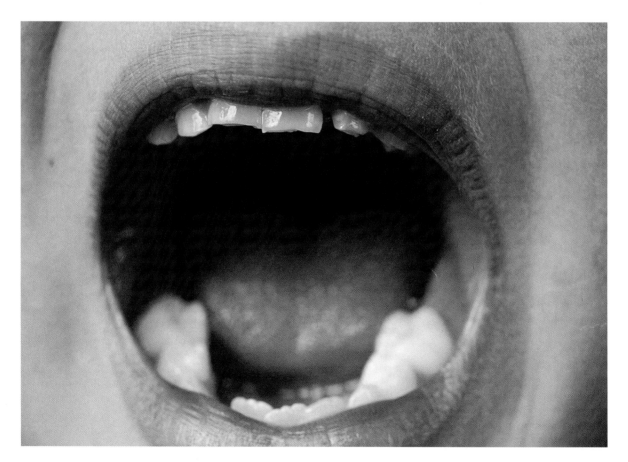

The mucous membranes trap many germs that get in through your nose and mouth. This keeps them from getting deeper into your body and making you sick.

What Causes Strep Throat?

Strep throat is caused by **bacteria.**
Bacteria are tiny living things. They are
so small you need a **microscope** to see
them. This is what strep throat bacteria
look like through a microscope.

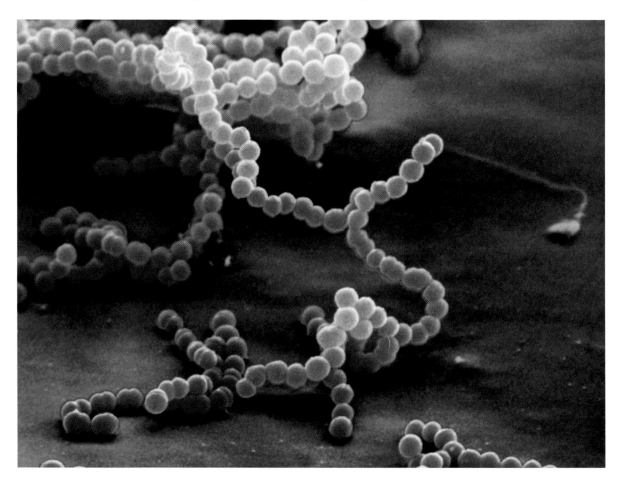

Some bacteria cause **infections** if they get inside your body. If strep bacteria get inside your body, they can make more bacteria. When this happens, you get sick.

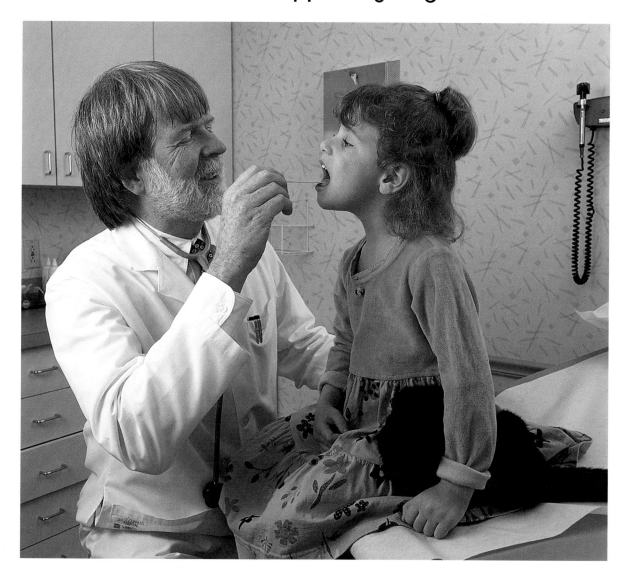

How Strep Throat Is Spread

Strep **bacteria** live in the nose and throat of a person who has strep throat. You can catch strep throat when someone with strep throat sneezes or coughs. Sneezing and coughing send the strep bacteria into the air.

If you breathe in the bacteria, you may get strep throat. If you catch strep throat, you should stay at home and rest so you don't spread it to others.

First Signs

Strep throat causes your throat to hurt a lot. You will probably also have a **fever.** That means the **temperature** of your body is hotter than usual.

Strep throat makes your throat look very red. It may have little white spots on it, too. These are signs of **infection.**

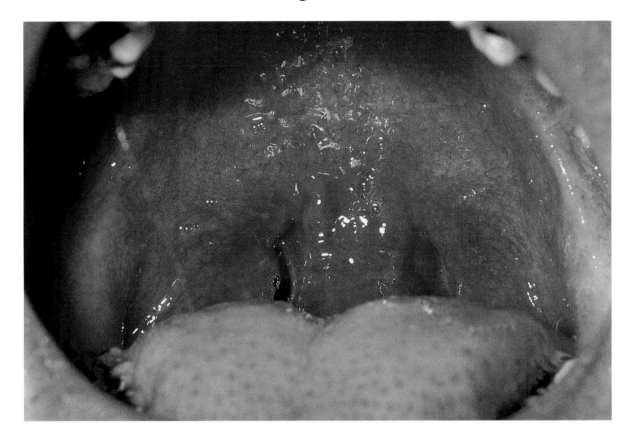

Other Signs

Strep throat makes the back and sides of your throat **swell,** or puff up. This may make it hard to swallow food. It is easier to drink juice and eat soft foods like ice cream or yogurt.

People with strep throat may not feel like eating at all. And sometimes they might feel sick to their stomachs and throw up.

Sore Throats

Sore throats can be caused by many different kinds of **germs.** Many times sore throats are caused by the germ that causes colds.

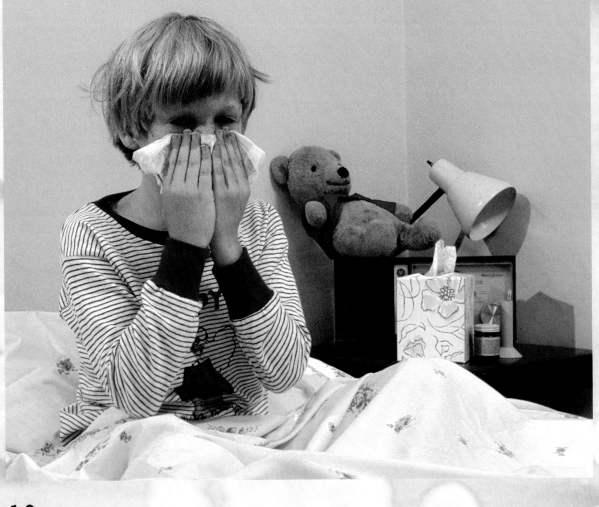

But strep throat is more serious than the sore throat you get with a cold. You need to go to a doctor to find out if you have strep throat.

Testing for Strep Throat

At the doctor's office, the doctor will softly touch the back of your throat with a **swab** like this one. Some of the **germs** in your throat will stick to the swab.

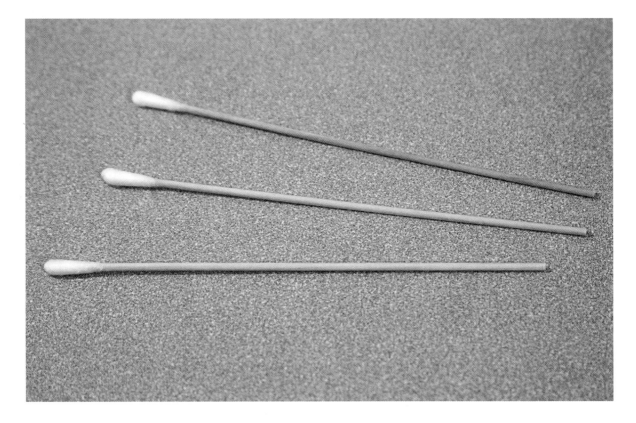

The doctor will then test the germs. If the test shows that the germs are strep **bacteria,** you have strep throat.

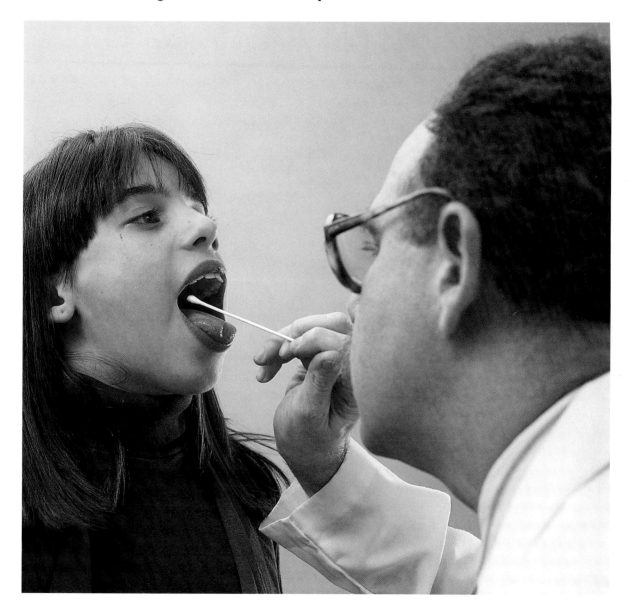

Treatment

If you have strep throat, your doctor will give you **antibiotics.** Antibiotics are a kind of medicine that kills **bacteria.**

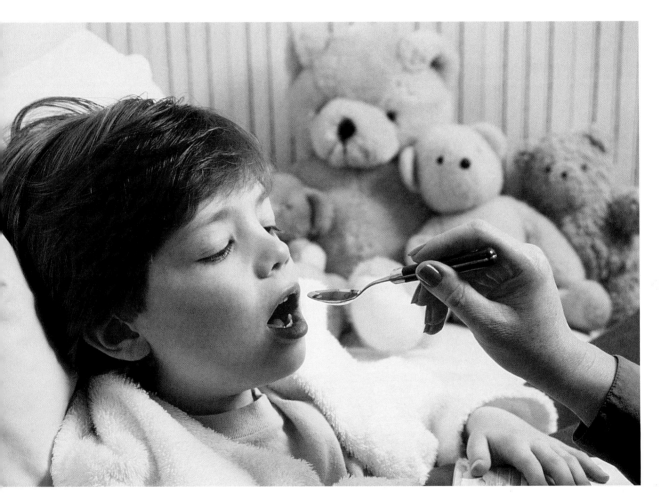

Getting lots of rest and drinking lots of water will help your body fight the **infection.** Eating ice cream or hot soup might make your throat feel better.

Getting Better

After taking **antibiotics** for one day
and one night, you won't be **infectious**
anymore. You can go back to school
then if you feel better. In a few days,
your sore throat will go away.

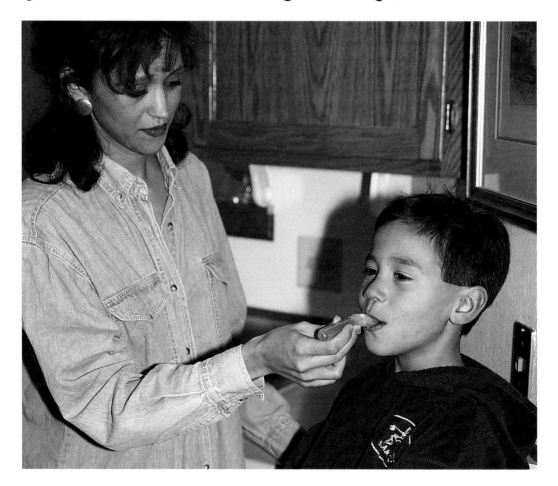

You must take the antibiotics for as long as your doctor tells you. If you stop taking them too soon, the **infection** can come back and get worse.

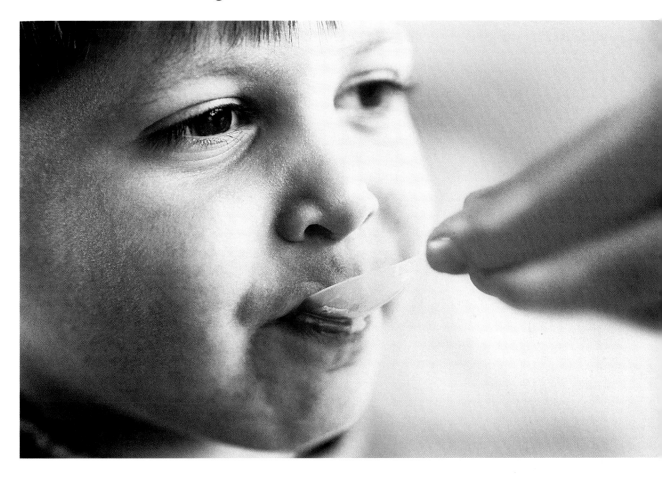

Avoiding Strep Throat

There is no medicine that will keep you from getting strep throat. If you are near a person with strep throat, you might catch it.

It is a good idea to wash your hands often if you are around people who are coughing and sneezing. The soap will kill **bacteria** and other **germs.**

Staying Healthy

Some doctors say you should get a new toothbrush after you have strep throat. Strep **bacteria** from your throat and mouth may be in your old toothbrush. Using it could give you strep throat again.

It is important to stay healthy. Eating good food, getting enough sleep, and exercising can help you stay healthy.

Think about It!

John has a sore throat and a **fever.** His family thinks he might have strep throat. How can they find out if John has strep throat?*

Jeff's sister, Pam, has strep throat. Pam has been taking **antibiotics** for four days. Can Jeff catch strep throat from Pam?*

*Read page 30 to find out.

Answers

Page 28

John will need to go to a doctor. The doctor will do a test to find out if strep **bacteria** are causing his sore throat.

Page 29

Pam has been taking **antibiotics** for four days, so she is not **infectious** anymore. Jeff cannot catch strep throat from Pam now.

Stay Healthy and Safe!

1. Always tell an adult if you feel sick or think there is something wrong with you.

2. Never take any medicine unless it is given to you by an adult you trust.

3. Remember, the best way to stay healthy and safe is to eat good food, drink lots of water, keep clean, exercise, and get lots of sleep.

Glossary

antibiotic   medicine that kills bacteria

bacteria   tiny living things that can make you sick if they get in your body

fever   when the temperature of your body becomes hotter than usual

germ   very tiny thing that can make you sick if it gets in your body

infection   sickness that can spread from one person to another

infectious   can be passed from one person to another and can make you sick

microscope   machine that makes very small things look big enough to see

mucous membrane   sticky inside of the nose and throat

swab   small stick with a cotton tip

swell   get bigger

temperature   measure of how hot or cold something is

Index

More Books to Read

Rowan, Kate. *I Know How We Fight Germs.* Cambridge, Mass.: Candlewick Press, 1999.

Royston, Angela. *Clean and Healthy.* Chicago: Heinemann Library, 1999.

Saunders-Smith, Gail. *The Doctor's Office.* Minnetonka, Minn.: Capstone Press, 1998.